D0991840

DISCARDED BY THE
URBANA FREE LIBRARY

	DATE DUE	
AUG 10 2012		
JUL 27 2013		

The Urbana Free Library

To renew materials call
217-367-4057

Learning Chinese
Through Stories and Activities

Belinda Yun-ying Louie
University of Washington Tacoma

Pictures by **Aki Sogabe**

BOOK PUBLISHERS NETWORK

9/10

Book Publishers Network
P.O. Box 2256
Bothell • WA • 98041
PH • 425-483-3040

Text copyright © 2007 by Belinda Y. Louie
Illustration copyright © 2007 by Aki Sogabe

All rights reserved. No part of this book may be reproduced, stored in, or introduced into a retrieval system, or transmitted in any form, or by any means (electronic, mechanical, photocopying, recording, or otherwise) without the prior written permission of the publisher.

10 9 8 7 6 5 4 3 2

Printed in the United States of America

    LCCN: 2007932344
    ISBN10: 1-887542-54-X
    ISBN13: 978-1-887542-54-X

    Interior Layout: Stephanie Martindale

Permission to copy activity pages for personal use only.
Evergreen Chinese Educational Resources Series
Series Editors: Douglas Louie, M.D., Ph.D., D.Min. and Belinda Louie, Ph.D.

CONTENTS

NOTES TO PARENTS AND TEACHERS

Learning Chinese is more than acquiring the language skills. A competent Chinese language learner understands the values and the cultures of the people who speak the language. Stories are the desired tools for conveying the cultural values, especially tales about outstanding children who later became important historical figures. The characters' exemplary behaviors are recorded to inspire children to behave likewise in their daily living. The stories in this book provide powerful images of courage and ingenuity, showing young readers how the characters feel, reason, and act. It is my hope that children can compare their thinking and actions with those of the traditional characters. During the process of reflection and discussion, children will develop a better understanding of themselves and the values embedded in the stories.

The bilingual texts in this book serve both advanced and novice Chinese language learners. The advanced learners can read the Chinese versions on their own and read the English versions to check their understanding of the texts. Beginning learners can study the key Chinese vocabulary items and read the English versions to enjoy the story. Parents and teachers should read and discuss the stories with both groups of learners. The book sharing can start by having children describe the customs and situations in the stories. They can then discuss how their experiences and family customs are similar to or different from the situations portrayed in the stories. Parents and teachers should support children to see that there is a range of customs and beliefs within the Chinese culture and that people from various cultures may share similar customs and beliefs. The activities associated with each story, aim to provide processing time for children to deepen their understanding of the values and to practice their Chinese language skills.

The stories can be used as teaching tools to learn the Chinese language and to understand the Chinese cultures. The paper-cut illustrations are for children to color. Above all, the stories are here for all to cherish and to enjoy.

ABOUT THE AUTHOR

Belinda Y. Louie is a professor of Education at the University of Washington Tacoma. She was a classroom teacher in Washington and California. In 2007, Dr. Louie received the Virginia Hamilton Essay Award for her contribution to multicultural juvenile literature. She also established the Professor Belinda Y. Louie Endowed Collection of Children's Literature for the University of Washington Library system. Professor Louie has served on numerous national children's and young adult literature projects. She led a 1999 People to People delegation of children's literature to China. Her scholarship focuses on literacy development, including K-12 students' responses to literature, language learning, and juvenile literature.

ABOUT THE ILLUSTRATOR

Working in the Pacific Northwest since 1978, Aki Sogabe has made her work known not only through her original paper cut designs, but also through the translation of her pieces into large public artworks. She has made over 2000 original paper cut designs in her 29-year career. Her work is in major collections, including the Mitsubishi International Corporation of Tokyo and Seattle, the University of Washington Tacoma, the University of Oregon, the Pike Place Market and the Wing Luke Asian Museum, Seattle. She is the illustrator of *Kogi*, *Orange in Golden Mountain*, *The Laziest Boy*, *The Loyal Cat*, and *The Hungriest Boy in the World*.

WEIGH AN ELEPHANT

General Cao received an elephant as a gift. He looked at that huge animal. He wondered how heavy it was. When he asked his servants for ways to weigh the elephant, nobody seemed to know how to do it.

"I have a way to weigh the elephant," said his 6-year-old son Cao Cong.*

Cao Cong asked the servants to load the elephant onto a boat. It was not an easy task. When the elephant put its first foot down, the boat rocked so much that it almost flipped over. With much shouting and pushing, the elephant finally was in the boat. Cao Cong quickly marked the water level at the side of the boat.

After bringing the elephant back on shore, Cao Cong asked the servants to load the boat with rocks until the water rose to the mark that he made earlier.

"Enough," Cao Cong told the servants to stop. "I think we have enough rocks. Go and weigh the rocks. We can find out how heavy the elephant is by measuring the weight of the rocks."

Cao Cong was the youngest son of General Cao Cao in the early 3rd century. Although Cao Cong died when he was only thirteen, his cleverness in problem-solving has inspired many generations of children. * In this book, all the characters' names start with their family names following the Chinese practice.

称大象

曹操将军收到一份礼物，一头"大象"，他看着这巨大的动物，心想它有多重呢？他问士兵们有什么办法可以给大象称重量，没有人知道该怎么做。

"我有个办法。" 曹操的小儿子曹冲大声说。

曹冲叫士兵们把大象牵到船上，这可不容易，当大象一脚踏上船头时，船开始剧烈的摇晃，士兵们又喊又推，大象最终上了船。曹冲立刻在船边做了个水位记号。

等到把大象牵回到岸上，曹冲又命令士兵们挑石头到船上，直到水位达到刚才的记号为止。"够了，"曹冲叫大家停下，"我想石头够了。去称出这些石头的重量，我们就能估计出大象的重量。"

曹冲是3世纪初曹操将军的小儿子，他虽然只活到13岁，可是他善于解决难题的聪明才智，一直流传给后代的孩子们作一个好榜样。

Vocabulary:

大象，重量，船，石头

Question for Reflection:

If you were going to describe Cao Cong to a friend, how would you describe him? What qualities does he have that you admire?

Activity: Tangram 七巧板

Tangram is an ancient Chinese moving piece puzzle, consisting of 7 geometric shapes. The objective is to form a specific shape with seven pieces. The shape has to contain all the pieces, which may not overlap. What kind of animal can you make using the tangram pieces? Make a copy of the tangram on page 41. Carefully cut out the large square. Then cut out the individual shapes. Color and arrange the puzzle pieces to make different designs. Can you make a boat, an elephant, and a soldier?

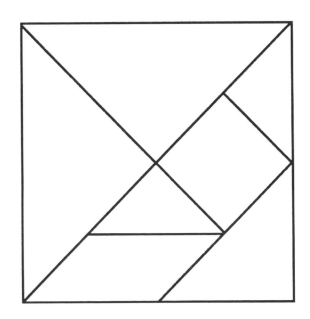 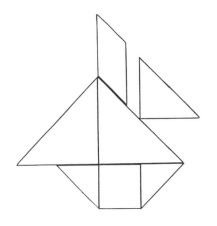 

WHICH PEAR TO PICK?

Kong Rong and his 3 older brothers reported their morning lessons to their father. A basket of golden pears sat on Father's desk. Kong Rong could hardly wait to bite into one of those crispy and sweet pears.

"My sons, go ahead and take a pear for yourself."

Kong Rong almost extended his hand to grab a pear. He stopped when he remembered Father always taught him and his brothers to honor people who were older. He quickly put his hands behind his back to wait for his turn. When he looked up, he caught the eyes of his eldest brother.

"Father, I suggest that Rong should go first this time. He is the youngest, and he always has to go last."

Kong Rong could hardly believe his ears. The eldest brother wanted him, the youngest, to go first. His eye was already on the biggest pear in the basket. Instead, he picked up the smallest.

"Why don't you pick a big one?" asked Father.

Kong Rong said, "I am the youngest, so I should get a small pear. My older brothers can have the bigger ones."

Kong Rong (153-208) was a famous scholar. It was believed that he was a descendant of the Confucius. This story of picking the smallest pear took place when Kong Rong was 4 years old.

拿哪一只梨呢？

孔融和三个哥哥在向父亲讲述早上的功课，一篮子漂亮的梨就放在父亲的桌子上，孔融忍不住想咬一口那又鲜又甜的梨子。

"孩子们，去自己拿一只梨吃吧。"

孔融正要伸手时，他想到父亲总是教导他们要尊重年龄大的人，他马上将手放到背后等着别人先拿。他抬头正好看到大哥的眼睛。

"父亲，我建议这回让孔融先拿，他最小，每次总是排在最后一个。"

孔融不能相信自己的耳朵，大哥愿意让他这个最小的弟弟先拿。他的眼睛、盯着篮子里最大的梨，最后，他决定拿了最小的一只。

"你为什么不拿一只大的呢？" 父亲问。

孔融说："我是最小的，应该拿小梨，哥哥们比我大，可以拿大梨。"

孔融（153-208），着名学者，传说是孔子的后代，这个"孔融让梨"的故事发生时，他只有四岁。

Vocabulary:

梨, 父亲, 哥哥, 最小

Question for Reflection:

Will you act like Kong Rong if you face the same situation? Why or why not?

Activity: Chinese Paper Cut 剪纸

Chinese papercutting is an ancient art form that has existed for thousands of years. People use knives or scissors to make various designs such as animals, flowers, and people. The paper cuts can be used as window or wall decorations. You can practice this special Chinese art form using the enlarged patterns of the pears and the basket on this page. Make a copy; then cut out pieces of pears of different sizes. Then, you can have your own basket of pears.

THE LOST BALL

After spending the whole morning studying the Chinese classics inside the classroom with Teacher Li, Wen Yenbo and his friends enjoyed a game of kick-ball in the east garden.

"Look what I can do," Dong Dong shouted over his shoulder while kicking the ball all the way to the old oak tree at the far side of the garden.

The ball fell into a tree hole. The children could not get the ball out. Their arms were too short. The sticks they found were too short. They tried and tried. None of the sticks was long enough to tilt the ball out. Each time, when it was almost within the reach of the stick, the ball seemed to roll further into the bottom of the hole.

"I have an idea." Wen Yenbo ran to get a wooden bucket. He quickly scooped water from the big cistern outside the kitchen. He poured water inside the tree hole; slowly, the ball floated upward on the rising water. Dong Dong picked up the ball. With a loud cheer, the boys ran back to the garden for another round of kick ball.

Wen Yenbo was an important government official in the 11th century. He served four emperors and was well respected during his time.

丢失的球

　　跟着李老师在教室里学了整个上午的古文之后，文彦博和他的伙伴们在花园里玩起了踢球游戏 。

　　"看我的。"东东回头大叫着将球远远地踢向花园另一边的老橡树。

　　球掉进了树洞。孩子们想拿出球，可是手臂太短，找来的树枝也都太短了。他们试啊试，没有一根树枝能触到球，相反，每次就快碰到球的时候，球好象都会向洞底滑去。

　　"我有办法。"文彦博跑去拿了一只木桶，从厨房外的大缸里舀满了水，他把水灌进树洞，慢慢地，球就随着上升的水浮了上来。东东拿到了球。孩子们大声欢呼着，又回花园玩踢球了。

文彦博 11 世纪时中国的政府官员，辅佐过四代皇帝，备受敬重。

Vocabulary:

花园, 踢球, 树洞, 游戏

Question for Reflection:

What do you think is the most admirable quality of Wen Yenbo?

Activity: Shuttlecock (Jian zi 毽子)

Shuttlecock is a traditional game that Chinese children love to play. One can play the game alone or with several friends. One player first tosses the jian zi into the air and then kicks it with his or her foot, knee, or heel. Players continue kicking the jian zi, not allowing it to touch the ground, no hands allowed. You can make your own jian zi using 4 artificial feathers, a piece of circular cardboard about one and a quarter inch in diameter, a piece of cellophane that is of the same size as the cardboard, and a piece of bolt washer.

1. Attach the feathers to the cellophane with glue.
2. Glue the base of the cellophane onto the cardboard.
3. Glue the bolt washer to the bottom of the whole unit.

COUNTING ON XUEN GUAN

Bandits surrounded and attacked the Town of Xiang, demanding food and money. The mayor of the town gathered all the officials to find a plan to save the town.

"Who can fight his way out to contact the Emperor's army at the other side of the mountain?" asked the mayor.

"Father, may I go?" Everyone was shocked when they heard the voice of Xuen Guan, the 13-year-old daughter of the mayor. Xuen Guan had been taking martial arts, horse-riding, and sword lessons since she could walk. Nevertheless, how could a young girl withstand the bandit's horde?

Many men were touched by Xuen Guan's courage. A group soon gathered to join her. They fought fearlessly through the enemy camp to reach the Emperor's army. The general immediately dispatched soldiers to rescue the citizens in the Town of Xiang. The town welcomed Xuen Guan back and praised her for her willingness to risk her life to save others.

Xuen Guan was a brave youth living around 280 A.D. Chinese people love to tell her story of courage.

依靠荀灌

　　土匪为抢夺食物和钱财围攻襄城，襄城太守召集所有官员商讨救城的方法。

　　"谁能杀出一条路联系山那边的皇帝的军队呢？"太守问大家。

　　"父亲，我可以去吗？"当大家听到太守13岁的女儿荀灌的声音时都愣住了。荀灌从学步开始就练习武术、骑马和各种兵器，然而，怎能让一个小女孩去面对土匪呢？

　　许多人被荀灌的勇敢所感动，一支队伍很快聚集在荀灌周围来支持她。他们英勇战斗，穿过敌人的营地，找到了皇帝的军队。将军立即派兵解救了襄城的百姓。全城的人都在城门欢迎荀灌，赞扬她舍命救他人的精神。

荀灌是东晋时期的少年英雄，她十三岁就率兵勇敢战斗，解救了全城的百姓。

Vocabulary:

土匪, 救城, 勇敢, 军队

Question for Reflection:

Why does Xuen Guan's father allow her to go on such a dangerous mission?

Activity: Chinese Go Game (Weiqi 围棋)

Go is a game of surrounding your opponent's territory and preventing yourself from being blocked. The game is played by two players (one with black stones and one with white stones), who take turns placing a stone or a game piece on the vacant intersections of a 19x19 board. Beginning players can use a smaller grid of 13 x 13. Stones of the same color connected to one another by the lines on the board form a *unit*. A stone or a group of stones can be removed if it is tightly surrounded by stones of the opposing color. The goal is to control a larger area than that of the other player by putting one's stones in ways that they can not be captured and removed. The game ends by counting the number of the opponent's stones that have been captured. There is a 19X19 grid on page 42.

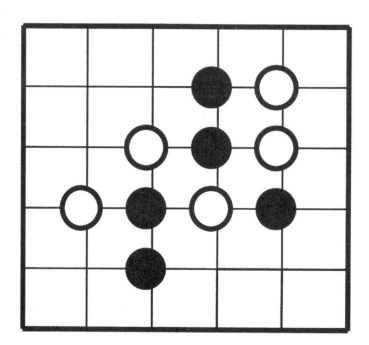

THE ARTIST, GU KAI ZHI

Looking outside the window, Gu Kai Zhi lost himself in the beauty of the summer garden. His neighbors always wondered how a young boy could sit still and stare at the trees, leaves, and flowers for such a long time. Little did they know that where they saw only twisting branches, the young Gu saw how a tree stretched its arms and legs to express its strength and character. In the bushy bamboo grove, he felt the exuberance of the dancing shadows of the pointed leaves. The peonies, voluptuous and fragrant, drew him in with their pink, yellow, red, and white blooms.

Gu Kai Zhi did not notice when his father came into the study. "My son, what do you plan to put on the paper today?"

"The song birds. Father, do you see how those birds flutter their wings when they touch the peonies?"

When his father took young Gu to official banquets, he again took in the movement of the people, the details of their elaborate gowns, and the flow of their elegant sleeves. In his mind, he always envisioned how lines connected together to produce shapes, movements, patterns, and even emotions.

Gu Kai Zhi (344-406 A.D.) was a very well-known artist. His work, the *Admonitions Scroll,* can be seen in the British Museum in London.

画家顾恺之

望着窗外，顾恺之被夏天的花园所吸引，别人总是好奇为什么这孩子老是喜欢盯着树木、树叶、和花朵。其实他们不知道，在众人眼里只是枝叶的东西，在少年的顾恺之眼中，却是树木伸出手臂来展示力量和个性。在茂密的竹林中，他感受到竹叶身影在跳舞时的愉快。牡丹花高贵而芳香，用粉红、黄色、红色和白色的花朵来向他招手。

"今天你打算画什么呀？"顾恺之不知道父亲何时来到了书房。

"小莺歌。父亲，你见到这些小鸟儿在牡丹花上是怎样抖动翅膀吗？"

当父亲带年幼的顾恺之参加宴会时，他惯常喜欢观察人物，仕女们身穿的精美衣袍，他们高雅的柔柔丝袖。在顾恺之的脑海中，他不断地想象如何用线条把外形、动作、图案，甚至感情表达出来。

顾恺之 346-407，著名画家，很小就博览群书，才华横溢。

Vocabulary:

翅膀, 线条, 图案, 表达

Question for Reflection:

How did Gu Kai Zhi's thoughtful observations of his surroundings help him as an artist?

Activity: Chinese Fan 扇子:

Chinese fans are both functional and decorative. Poets and artists always print poems in beautiful calligraphy and paint sceneries, flowers, and birds on the spread of the fan.

1. Enlarge the rectangular box with the garden design on page 43, color the garden design with water color or color pencils, and cut out the rectangular box and fold accordion style.

2. Open top, fold up bottom tap and staple to form handle. You can make a tassel and staple it onto the handle.

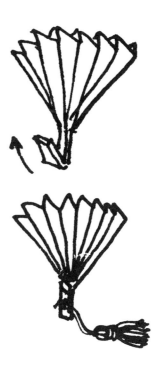

A DONKEY FOR MY FATHER

Governor Xuan invited many distinguished guests to his mansion for a wonderful night of celebration. Mr. Zhuge decided to bring his son, Zhuge Kai, to this festive event.

When all the guests were seated, a servant brought a donkey into the banquet hall. When the donkey came close, both father and son were shocked to see Mr. Zhuge's name written on a tag hung around the neck of the donkey. What a cruel joke!

Zhuge Kai knew that people always made fun of his father's long face. His father was a kind and gentle man. People had no right to embarrass his father publicly on this joyous occasion.

Zhuge Kai had an idea. He quickly walked to the entry table where brushes and ink were there for guests to sign their names on the red cloth. He took the brush and added a few words to the donkey tag. Instead of "Zhuge Zhi Yu," now the tag read "Zhuge Zhi Yu's donkey."

Governor Xuan was deeply impressed by how Zhuge Kai used his wit to turn shame into triumph. He awarded the donkey to Mr. Zhuge.

Zhuge Kai was a famous general in the time of the Three Kingdoms (around 400 A.D.). He was known for his literary accomplishments and his martial arts skills.

给父亲的驴

　　孙权邀请了许多贵宾到他的官邸举办庆祝晚会，诸葛子瑜决定带儿子诸葛恪一起参加。

　　当所有客人就座后，一个佣人牵了一头驴来到宴会厅。当驴走近时，诸葛先生和儿子都很惊奇，发现驴的脖子上有一个标签，上面写着诸葛先生的名字。太让人难堪的玩笑了！

　　诸葛恪知道人们常常取笑父亲的长脸。父亲是一个善良仁慈的人，人们没有权利在这样的公众场合令他尴尬。

　　诸葛恪有一个主意，他快速走到来宾签名放有毛笔和墨水的台子前，用毛笔在驴的标签上加了几个字，原来的"诸葛子瑜"，变成为"诸葛子瑜的驴"。

　　孙权很欣赏诸葛恪能以机智幽默把羞辱变为胜利，便将那头驴奖赐给诸葛子瑜。

诸葛恪：三国时的名将，诸葛亮的亲侄，文武双全，才华出众。

Vocabulary:

贵宾, 驴, 尴尬, 机智幽默

Question for Reflection:
What were some other ways that Zhuge Kai could have responded to the embarrassing situation?

Activity: Chinese Writing 汉字
Chinese characters have evolved over a long period of time, transforming from pictographs to the more abstract characters that we use today. Can you match each pictograph with its character?

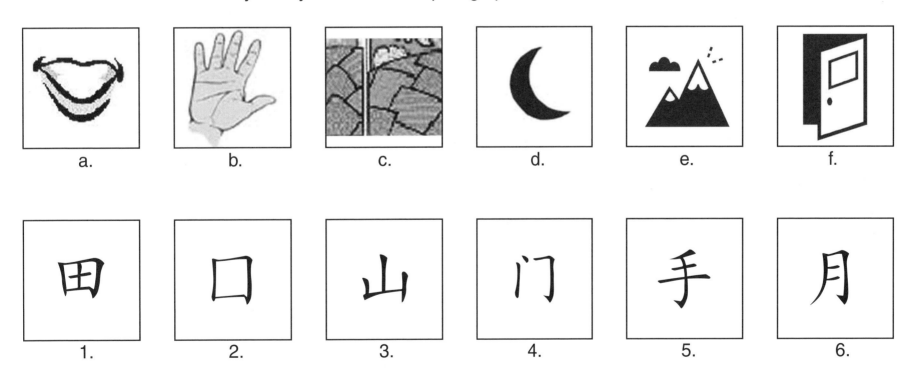

a.　　b.　　c.　　d.　　e.　　f.

田　　口　　山　　门　　手　　月

1.　　2.　　3.　　4.　　5.　　6.

Answer key: a-2, b-3, c-5, d-6, e-1, and f-4

TURNING AN IRON ROD INTO A NEEDLE

Li Bai skipped school to fish at the river. He found an old woman sitting outside a small house not far from the bank. She was rolling an iron rod against a piece of flat stone on a tree stump. Li Bai stopped and watched.

"Good morning, grandmother. What are you doing with the rod?" Li Bai was getting curious.

"I want to turn it into a needle," replied the old woman.

"Can you really turn a rod into a needle?" Li Bai could not help but rub his own hands, imagining the callouses that would grow on his hands if he was the one who was rolling the rod.

"Young man, everything takes time. If I keep on sharpening this rod against the stone plate, it will become a needle one of these days."

Li Bai had never thought about putting his energy into any job that required so much time and hard work. He looked at the old grandmother with the iron rod and pictured a shining needle. Slowly, Li Bai turned around and walked up the path to the school house.

Li Bai is one of the most famous poets of China in the 8th century. His poems have touched the hearts of generations of Chinese people.

铁杵磨成针

　　李白逃学到河边钓鱼，他看到一位老奶奶坐在岸边不远的小屋前，正用木桩上的石板磨一根铁棒，李白停下来看着。

　　"早上好，奶奶。你磨铁棒做什么？"李白好奇地问。

　　"我要把它变成一根针。"老奶奶说。

　　"你真的能把铁棒磨成针？"李白不自觉地用手比划着，心想如果换他磨铁棒的话，手上一定长出老茧了。

　　"年轻人，做任何事情都要花时间的。只要坚持磨下去，总有一天它会变成针的。"

　　李白从来没想过集中精力来做任何需要付出时间和努力的事情。他看着老奶奶的铁棒，想象着它变成了一根闪亮的针。慢慢地，李白转身沿小路返回学校去。

李白是中国8世纪时最著名的诗人之一，他的诗打动无数中国人的心。

Vocabulary:

铁棒，逃学，坚持，努力

Question for Reflection:

Why did Li Bai decide to go back to the school house after talking with the old woman?

Activity: Chinese Seals 印章

A Chinese seal is a stamp with Chinese characters used as a signature on documents, contracts, or art. Seals are often used in Chinese calligraphic works or Chinese paintings to document authorship. We can use a potato stamp to make Chinese name seals. You will need a potato, a sharp knife, paint, paper, and a shallow dish.

Method:

You can use tracing paper to trace the Chinese name seal (which means "Distinguished Youth") on this page. You can also design your own name seal in English, similar to the one shown on this page. Wash the potato, and cut it in half. On the cut face of the potato, put the tracing paper with the design. Using the knife to carve, cut away the potato surrounding the lines, so that the line protrudes about half a centimeter (1/5 inch). You can now use this shape as a stamp. Put the paint in a shallow dish, so you can 'ink' the stamp in the paint. Cover the potato stamp you have made with color from the water-based paint. Now you can use your seal on a clean piece of paper.

HIDE-AND-SEEK

"Ten, nine, eight …," Sima Guang turned toward the wall as he quickly counted down. "Here I come!"

The garden was a great place for playing hide-and-seek. Children could squeeze their bodies inside the cracks of the miniature decorative rock mountains. They could hide behind the big pillars of the summer pavilion. They could make themselves invisible in the dense bamboo grove. Some even climbed up the willow tree next to the lotus pond. They could also tip-toe into the peony bushes as long as they were careful not to destroy any of the gardener's precious blooms.

Splish! Splash!

"Xiao Bai fell into the *gang*!"

The giant ceramic water vat sat next to the tallest miniature rock mountain. Xiao Bai must have lost his balance when he tried to climb to the top of the fixture. Sima Guang sensed that there was no time to lose. He quickly grabbed a huge rock and hit the side of the cistern. He hit the side hard until the *gang* cracked open and water gushed out. Sima Guang stopped and reached in to pull his coughing friend out of danger.

Sima Guong (1019-1086 A.D.) was a famous politician, historian, and author. He was a gentle and humble person.

捉迷藏

　　"十、九、八…"司马光对着墙快速地倒数数字，"我来了！"

　　花园是玩捉迷藏的好地方，孩子们可以缩进假山的缝隙中；可以躲藏在凉亭的柱子后面；可以隐身在稠密的竹林里让人看不见；还有的爬到莲花池边的柳树上；他们还可以踮着脚悄悄地走在牡丹花丛中，只要小心不要踏坏了园丁的宝贝花朵。

　　扑通！扑通！

　　"小白掉进水缸了！"

　　大水缸放在高高的假山旁边，小白一定是在爬假山的时候失去了平衡，跌进水缸里。司马光感到不能耽误时间，他快速拿起一块大石头砸向水缸边。他用力地砸，直到水缸裂开，水泻了出来。司马光伸手拉出咳嗽的小白，他终于脱险了。

司马光，1019-1086，着名政治家、史学家、散文芳家，为人温良诲谦恭，刚正不阿，受人景仰。

Vocabulary:

躲藏， 假山， 耽误， 平衡

Question for Reflection:

If you were one of the children in the game, what would you have done when Xiao Bai fell into the water?

Activity: Chinese Shadow Puppetry 皮影

In China, shadow puppet theater was a form of popular entertainment in open markets, where crowds of people from all walks of life gathered to watch performances based on legends and popular tales. The puppets were carved out of translucent parchment and painted in colors. The heads were detachable from the eleven separate pieces which made up the body. Puppeteers used control rods to move the head and the body of the figures. The stage for the shadow is a white cloth screen on which the shadows are projected. You can make your own puppets by making copies of the figures provided on pages 44 and 45. You can use a brad to connect the head and the body of the puppet figure. You can tape plastic straws at the back of the head and the body to move the puppet.

TI YING TO THE RESCUE

"It is a pity that I only have 5 daughters. None of them can help me when I am in trouble," Dr. Chunyu sighed as the guards took him away in front of his weeping daughters. One of the Emperor's relatives was very sick. He died soon after Dr. Chunyu's house visit. When the Emperor received the news, he ordered the doctor thrown into the imperial prison.

Little Ti Ying, the youngest daughter, decided to go to the capital with her father. The journey was long and hard. Ti Ying had never left her home before. Now, she had to walk on uneven paths, into swamps, and through forests. Hunger and thirst only added to her determination to save her father.

When she arrived at the capitol, she pleaded with a scribe to write a letter for her to the Emperor. In the letter, she begged the Emperor to free her father. She was willing to serve his sentence for him. Brave Ti Ying took the letter to the palace guards. When the Emperor read the letter, he was so moved by Ti Ying's love for her father and her courage to appeal to the emperor, he gave the order to set the doctor free.

Ti Ying was the daughter of the famous doctor Chunyu Yi, living around 200 B.C.

缇萦救父

"可惜我只有五个女儿，在我危难的时候没有人能帮我。"淳于医生在叹息，侍卫把他从哭泣的女儿面前带走了。一位皇帝的近亲得了重病，在淳于意医生看过他之后不久就死了，当皇帝听了这个消息，下令将医生关入皇家大牢。

小缇萦，医生最小的女儿，决定跟父亲一起去京城，行程又长又艰辛，缇萦从来没有离开过家，现在她要走过崎岖的路，经过沼泽，还要穿越森林。饥饿和口渴只能更加坚定她救父亲的决心。

从她来到京城，她恳求一位文人替她写了一封信给皇上。信中，她央求皇上放了父亲，她愿意替父亲服刑。缇萦把信交给宫廷的侍卫，当皇上读了这封信，深深地被缇萦的孝心和勇敢所打动，下令释放了淳于医生。

缇萦，中国汉代时名医淳于意的小女儿，她因15岁时上书皇上解救父亲的孝行而留下了千古美名。

Vocabulary:

危难, 哭泣, 决心, 孝心

Question for Reflection:
Do you think it would be reasonable for Ti Ying to serve her father's sentence? Why or why not?

Activity: Terra Cotta Soldier Puppet 兵马俑

The Terra Cotta Warriors are important archeological excavations in China. They are life-sized sculptures created by Emperor Qin (3rd B.C.) as buried treasures in his tomb. The soldiers are replicas of what the imperial guard should look like in those days.

1. Make a copy of the soldier pattern on page 46 and 47. You will also need a paper bag.
2. Color the head and the body of the soldier.
3. Cut out the head and the body separately.
4. Glue the head on the folded base of the paper bag.
5. Glue the body on the side of the paper bag.
6. Adjust the body before you glue so that the head is right above the body.

WALKING TEN THOUSAND MILES

Sima Qian grew up in a family of historical scholars. His father was the Grand Librarian, managing the imperial library. Being a very diligent student, Sima Qian was very familiar with many ancient writings when he was 10 years old . The more he read, the more he yearned to visit the places and the monuments that were described in the scrolls.

"Father, I love reading in the quietness of the library, but the scripts make me wonder how the world really looks like outside these quiet walls," Sima Qian confided in his father. "May I take a tour around the country?"

To travel across the country was not an easy task. Father considered the hardship and the dangers that the young man would endure. He loved his son, and he knew that the trip would broaden Sima Qian's mind. After much preparation, Sima Qian finally started his journey when he was 20 years old. During his travels, he collected many useful first-hand historical records, verified many local legends, and visited monuments and the graves of the ancient kings.

Sima Qian (145-87 B.C.) was a famous historian. He authored the *Chronicles of the Chinese Dynasties* (*Shi Zhi*) which people still study today.

行万里路

司马迁成长在一个史学之家，他的父亲是一位著名的图书馆员，管理着皇家的图书馆。作为一名勤奋的学生，司马迁十岁的时候就熟读许多历史著作。他读的越多，就越渴望实地考察那些古书中提到的地方和历史遗迹。

"父亲，我喜欢在安静的图书馆看书，但书卷让我很想知道墙外的真实世界是什么样的。"司马迁向父亲吐露了心中的想法。"我能到全国各地去旅行吗？"

周游全国并不容易，父亲考虑到年轻人要忍耐的艰辛和危险，他爱他的儿子，他明白旅行会使司马迁的眼界开阔，经过认真准备，司马迁在二十岁的时候开始启程了。在旅程中，他收集了有价值的第一手历史记录，核实了许多地方传说，参观了历史遗迹和古代帝王的墓碑，这些资料后来成为了他的巨着《史记》的重要组成部分。

司马迁，公元前145-87，中国伟大的历史学家，巨著《史记》是他留给世界的一笔珍贵文化遗产。

Vocabulary:

图书, 历史, 考察, 遗迹

Question for Reflection:
What kinds of problems do you think that Sima Guong had to overcome when he traveled?

Activity: A Walk in the Country
China is a big country with many famous places. Make a copy of the pictures of the four important sites (Forbidden City in Beijing, the Great Wall of China, the Terra Cotta Tomb, and the skyline of Shanghai). On page 48 of this book you can cut out the pictures, and paste them on the map.

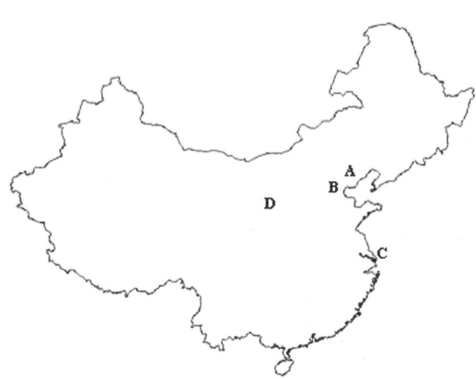

A. Forbidden City	B. Great Wall

C. Shanghai	D. Terra Cotta Soldier and Tomb

SUGGESTED READING LIST

Bateson-Hill, Margaret. (1996). *Lao Lao of Dragon Mountain*. New York: De Agostini Children's Books.

Chang, Monica. (1992). *The Mouse Bride*. Union City, CA: Pan Asian Publications.

Dean, Arlan. (2005). *Terra-cotta Soldiers: Army of Stones*. New York: Scholastic Press.

Ho, Monfong. (1996). *Maples in the Mist: Children's Poems from the Tang Dynasty*. New York: Lothrop, Lee and Shepard Books.

Louie, Ai-ling. (1982) *Yeh Shen: A Cinderella Story from China*. New York : Philomel Books

Partridge, Elizabeth. (2003). *Oranges on Golden Mountain*. New York: Puffin.

Pilegard, Virginia Walton. (2000). *The Warlord's Puzzle*. New York: Pelican.

San Souci, Robert D. (1998). *Fa Mulan*. New York: Hyperion.

Shepard, Aaron. (2001). *Lady White Snake: A Tale from Chinese Opera*. Union City, CA: Pan Asian.

Tompert, Ann. (1990). *Grandfather Tang's Story*. New York: Crown.

Young, Ed. (1989). *Lon Po Po: A Red Riding-hood story from China*. New York : Philomel Books.

Va, Leong. (1987). *A Letter to the King*. New York: HarperCollins.

Young, Ed. (1997). *Voices of the Heart*. New York: Scholastic Press.

BIBLIOGRAPHY

Borja, Coriinne. (1980). *Making Chinese Paper Cuts*. New York: Albert Whitman and Company.

Fung, Shiu-Ying. (1972). *Chinese Children's Games*. New York: A.R.T.S.

Kalman, Bobbie. (1989). *China: Culture, Land, People 3-Volumn Set*. Cincinnati, OH: Asia for Kids.

Krah, Maywan Shen, and Zhang, Hongbin. (1997). *D is for Doufu*. Fremont, CA: Shen's Books.

March, Benjamin. (1938). *Chinese Shadow-figure Plays and Their Making*. Detroit, MI: Puppetry Imprints.

Pen, Tan Huay. (2003). *Fun with Chinese Characters*. Cincinnati, OH: Infini Press.

Qian, Gonglin. (2004). *Chinese Fans: Artistry and Aesthetics*. San Francisco: Long River Press.

Shotwell, Peter; Yang, Huiren; and Chatterjee, Sangit. (2003). *Go: More Than a Game*. North Clarendon, VT: Tuttle Publishing.

Sun, Weizu. (2004). *Chinese Seals: Carving Authority and Creating History*. San Francisco: Long River Press.

Stalberg, Roberta Helmer. (1984). *China's Puppets*. San Francisco: China Books.

Tangram

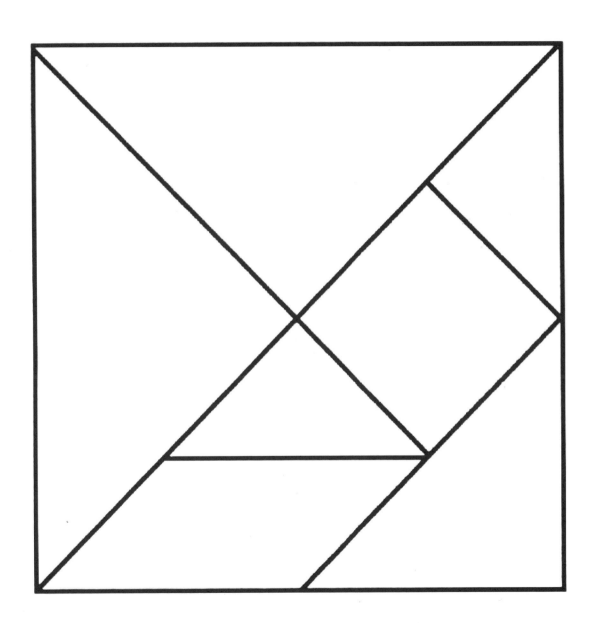

Go grid

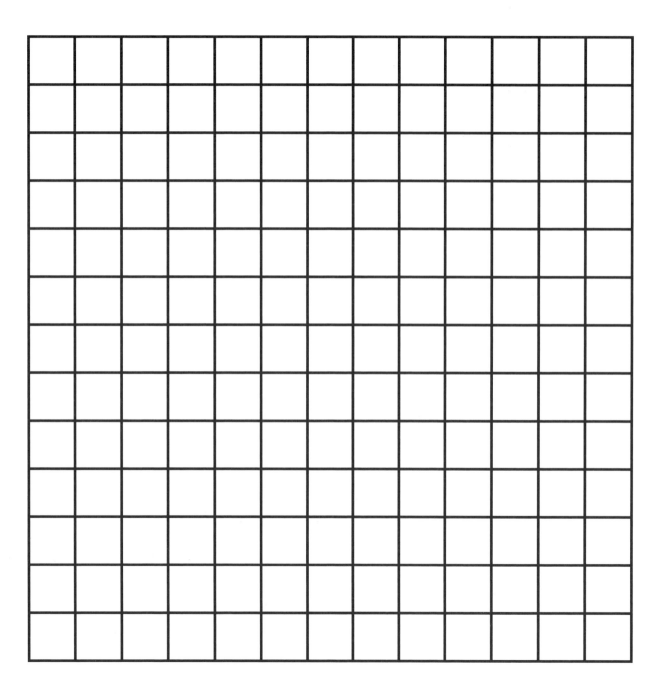

Fan

Shadow Puppets

Soldier

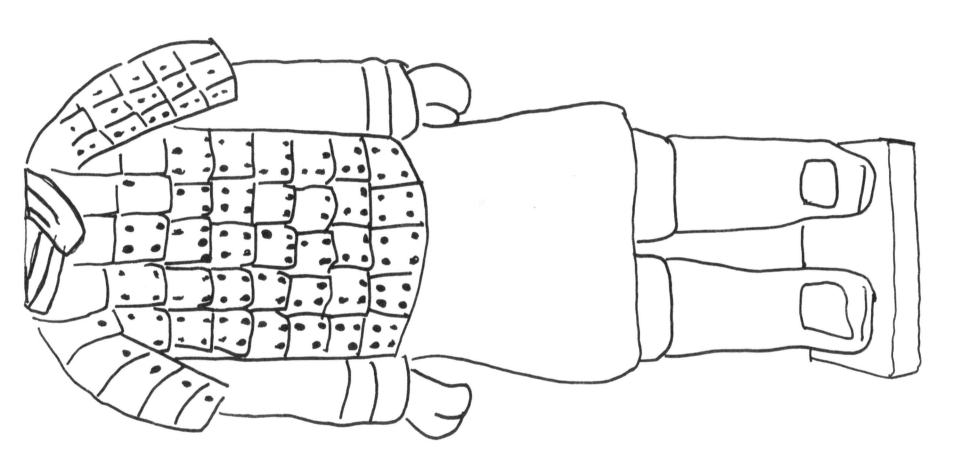

Map of China

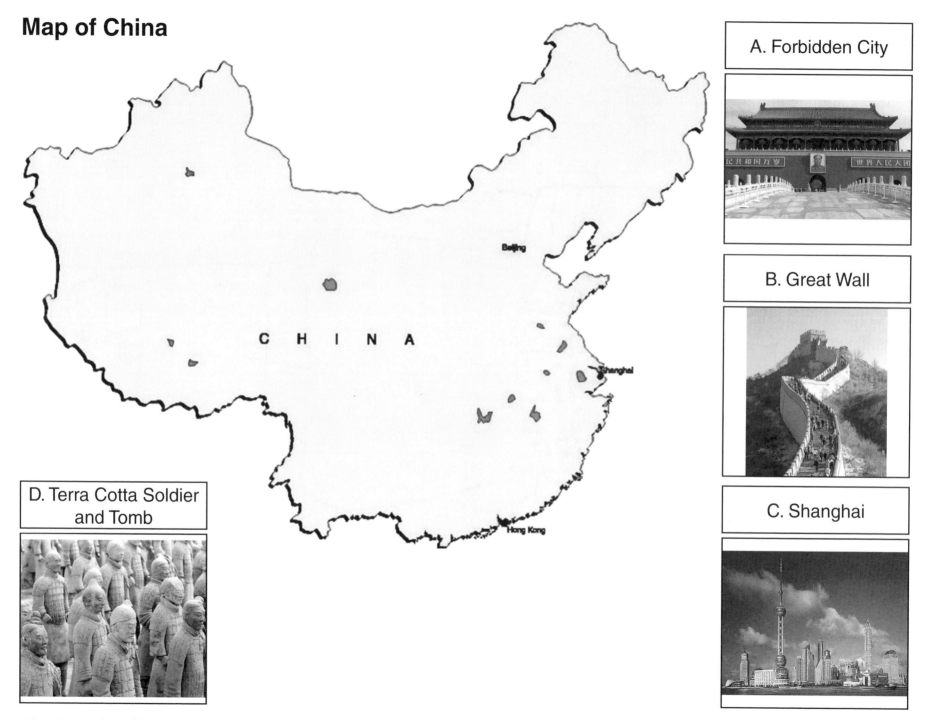

A. Forbidden City

B. Great Wall

C. Shanghai

D. Terra Cotta Soldier and Tomb

Beijing

CHINA

Shanghai

Hong Kong

9622